BOMB SQUAD!

MORE THAN 100 BOMB SHOT DRINKS

STERLING
New York

An Imprint of Sterling Publishing
387 Park Avenue South
New York, NY 10016

STERLING and the distinctive Sterling logo are registered trademarks of Sterling Publishing Co., Inc.

Book Design and Illustration by Jon Chaiet

ISBN 978-1-4549-0115-0

The drinks in this book are alcoholic in nature and meant to be consumed in moderation by adults of legal drinking age.

Distributed in Canada by Sterling Publishing
c/o Canadian Manda Group, 165 Dufferin Street
Toronto, Ontario, Canada M6K 3H6

Distributed in the United Kingdom by GMC Distribution Services
Castle Place, 166 High Street, Lewes, East Sussex, England BN7 1XU

Distributed in Australia by Capricorn Link (Australia) Pty. Ltd.
P.O. Box 704, Windsor, NSW 2756, Australia

For information about custom editions, special sales, and premium and corporate purchases, please contact
Sterling Special Sales at 800-805-5489 or specialsales@sterlingpublishing.com.

Printed in China

2 4 6 8 10 9 7 5 3 1

www.sterlingpublishing.com

BOMB SQUAD!

MORE THAN 100 BOMB SHOT DRINKS

PAUL KNORR

STERLING
New York

For my children:

Camryn, Colby, and Cooper

CONTENTS

First it was just a shot and a beer. A shot of whiskey followed by a beer to wash it down. At some point in the late 1890s or early 1900s this simple combination came to be known as a boilermaker. Along with the new name came a new way to drink it. Now, instead of chasing the whiskey with the beer, the whiskey was dropped *into* the beer and the entire mixture was consumed in a single gulp. If you did not consume it quickly enough, the beer would foam up and spill out of the glass. It became a test of skill and stamina.

Several variations of the boilermaker have sprung up over the years, but only a few have had any staying power. The Irish Car Bomb is one of those that has not only stood the test of time but has increased in popularity since its invention in the early 1980s. An Irish Car Bomb consists of a shot glass filled with half Irish whiskey and half Irish Cream liqueur dropped into a pint of Guinness. The name refers to both the Irish ingredients and to the troubled history of Ireland and the IRA. Legend has it that the drink was invented in a small bar in Norwich, Connecticut, by Charles Burke Cronin Oat in 1981. It's not clear if Mr. Oat was the bartender or the owner. Oat took a drink he had invented two years earlier called the IRA and dropped it into his glass of Guinness, shouting, "Bombs away!" Thus the Irish Car Bomb was born. For the next twenty years, the Irish Car Bomb and its cousins would spread throughout the nation, but they would stay in the background, coming out for Saint Patrick's Day or other special occasions. It would not be until the late 1980's that a bold new kind of beverage would literally *wake up* the realm of bomb style drinks.

Red Bull® was developed in Austria by Dietrich Mateschitz in 1987 based on a drink that was popular in Thailand at the time. The name came from taurine, an amino acid first discovered in bulls and known to boost energy and concentration. The drink was introduced in the United States in 1997 and quickly took off in popularity. Energy drinks are now the fastest growing segment of the American beverage market, going from $8 million in 2001 to $3 billion in 2006.

Long before Red Bull ever made its way to the U.S., the earlier Japanese and Thai versions were becoming a fad among late night revelers and club goers as a way to keep the party going into the early morning. By the time Red Bull came to the U.S., the idea of mixing an energy drink with alcohol had already been well established in Asia and Europe. The extra bit of American ingenuity came from combining our native bomb-style drinks with the new energy drink fad. The most famous result of this intercontinental mash-up is the Jäger Bomb—a shot of Jägermeister® dropped into a glass of Red Bull.

What follows in this book is a collection of drinks that includes the classic boilermaker drinks, the mixed-shot car-bomb–style drinks, the new energy bomb drinks, and new ones that build on the former drinks.

Each drink recipe in this book consists of two parts: the *shot* and the *drop*. The *shot* portion is the ingredients to be combined in a shot glass. The *drop* portion is what the shot is to be dropped into. When the two combine, you have a bomber drink!

The target glass that the shot will be dropped into should be a heavy-duty pint (½ liter) glass. As noted in all of the recipes, the glass should only be filled half way. This will prevent spillage and a messy overflow when the shot is dropped in.

A Note on Safety There are two physical hazards inherent to bomber drinks: chipped glassware and chipped teeth. Dropping one glass into another can result in the cracking, chipping, or breaking of one of the glasses. In general, drinking broken glass is not a good thing. Even if the glass does not chip or break, a shot glass banging into your teeth while you chug your drink down can lead to a chipped tooth and a visit to the dentist.

A simple way to prevent both of these is to use a plastic, disposable shot glass instead of a glass one. Another option is to use specialty glassware such as the Powerbomb brand bomb shot cups. Powerbomb cups have a 1-ounce inner cup and a 4-ounce outer cup combined into one piece of plastic, so there is no dropping of the shot because it's built right in.

Finally, these drinks can be powerful and should never be consumed by someone who will have to drive home. Don't let your night of car bombs turn into a car wreck.

Note: In the recipes in this book, the term "part" is used to indicate a rate of ingredients. One part is one measure, whether that be ounces, centiliters, or what have you. Two parts would be twice as much as one part.

GLOSSARY OF INGREDIENTS

Amaretto An Italian liqueur made from apricot kernels and seeds combined with almond extract steeped in brandy and sweetened with sugar syrup. *Amaretto* is Italian for "a little bitter."

Blackberry Liqueur A sweet blackberry-flavored liqueur usually 30–50 proof (15–25 percent alcohol) with added sugar.

Blue Curaçao A liqueur flavored with the dried peel of laraha citrus fruit which is related to the Valencia orange. The liqueur has an orange flavor and is artificially colored blue.

Bourbon An American form of whiskey made from at least 51 percent corn, with the remainder being wheat or rye and malted barley. It is distilled to no more than 160 proof (80 percent alcohol by volume) and aged in new charred white-oak barrels for at least two years. It must be put into the barrels at no more than 125 U.S. proof.

Brandy A liquor made from distilled wine (fermented grape juice) or other fermented fruit juice.

Coffee Liqueur *See* Tia Maria®

Cointreau® A fine, colorless, orange-flavored liqueur made from the dried skins of oranges grown on the island of Curaçao in the Dutch West Indies. The generic term for this type of liqueur is Curaçao; if it is re-distilled and clarified, it is called triple sec.

Crème Liqueurs Crème liqueurs are very sweet, with a single flavor that dominates.

> **Crème de Banana** Banana-flavored sweet liqueur.
>
> **Crème de Cacao (Dark)** Chocolate-flavored sweet liqueur that is dark brown in color.
>
> **Crème de Cacao (White)** Colorless, chocolate-flavored sweet liqueur.

Gin Gin begins as a neutral spirit. It is then re-distilled with or filtered through juniper berries and botanicals such as coriander seeds, cassia bark, orange peels, fennel seeds, anise, caraway, angelica root, licorice, lemon peel, almonds, cinnamon bark, bergamot, and cocoa; it is this secondary process that imparts to each gin its particular taste.

Godiva® Liqueur A neutral spirit–based liqueur flavored with Godiva® brand Belgian chocolate and other flavors. There are currently four types: milk chocolate, original chocolate, white chocolate, and mocha.

Grand Marnier® A French brand of orange-flavored liqueur (triple sec) with a brandy base.

Grenadine A sweet syrup made from pomegranate juice, containing little or no alcohol.

Hennessy A brand of cognac (distilled wine, or brandy) produced in Cognac, France.

Honey Liqueur (Bärenjäger) A German honey-flavored liqueur with a vodka base. Bärenjäger means "bear-hunter" in German.

Hypnotiq A 34-proof liqueur made from a blend of fruit juices, vodka, and cognac.

Irish Cream Liqueur A mocha-flavored whiskey and double-cream liqueur, combining Irish whiskey, cream, coffee, chocolate, and other flavors.

Jack Daniel's® A whiskey made in Tennessee that is perhaps the most famous whiskey made in America. The Jack Daniel's distillery in

Lynchburg, Tennessee, dates from 1875 and is the oldest registered distillery in the United States. Jack Daniel's® is made according to the sour-mash process, and by the "Lincoln County Process" of filtration through sugar maple charcoal before being aged in charred American oak casks.

Jägermeister® A complex, aromatic liqueur containing fifty-six herbs, roots, and fruits that has been popular in Germany since its introduction in 1935. In Germany, it is frequently consumed warm as an aperitif or after-dinner drink. In the United States it is widely popular as a chilled shooter.

Johnny Walker® Scotch A brand of Scotch whiskey owned by Diageo and originated in Kilmarnock, Ayrshire, Scotland.

Kahlúa A coffee-flavored liqueur with a rum base. Sugar and vanilla are added for flavor.

Licor 43® (Cuarenta y Tres) A yellow liqueur from Spain made from forty-three ingredients including fruit juices, vanilla, and other aromatic herbs and spices.

Limoncello A lemon liqueur traditionally made with Sorrento lemons in southern Italy.

Maraschino Liqueur A very sweet white cherry liqueur made from the marasca cherry of Dalmatia, Yugoslavia.

Melon Liqueur A pale green liqueur that tastes of fresh muskmelon or cantaloupe. The most famous brand, Midori®, is Japanese in origin and is produced by the Suntory Company in Mexico, France, and Japan.

Midori® A pale green, melon-flavored liqueur produced by Suntory in Japan, Mexico and France. Midori is Japanese for green.

Mozart® Black Chocolate Liqueur A dark-chocolate-and-vanilla-flavored liqueur.

Raspberry Liqueur A sweet raspberry-flavored liqueur usually 30–50 proof (15–25 percent alcohol) with added sugar.

Rum A liquor made from fermented and distilled sugar-cane juice or molasses. Rum has a range of flavors, from light and dry like a vodka to very dark and complex like a cognac.

Light Rum Clear in color and dry in flavor.

Spiced Rum The original flavored rum. Spiced rum consists of an amber rum with vanilla and cinnamon flavors added.

Rumple Minze® A 100-proof peppermint schnapps produced in Germany.

Sake A rice-based alcoholic beverage from Japan, commonly referred to as rice-wine. The process used to make sake is actually more like that used to make beer.

Sambuca An Italian liqueur flavored with anise and elderberry, produced in both clear ("white sambuca") and dark blue or purple ("black sambuca") versions.

Schnapps A liqueur distilled from grains, roots, or fruits. Real schnapps has no sugar or flavoring added, as the flavor should originate from the base material. Many syrupy, sweet fruit liqueurs are called schnapps, but they are not true schnapps because they have both sugar and flavorings added.

Scotch A whiskey made in Scotland from malted barley. The whiskey must be aged at least three years. Scotch can be further divided into single malt and blended. Single malt is scotch from a single batch of a single pot still at a single distillery. Blended scotch is scotch where the flavors of multiple batches from multiple distilleries are combined.

Sloe Gin A liqueur flavored with sloe berries and blackthorn fruit. It traditionally was made with a gin base with sugar added, but most modern versions use a neutral spirit base and add flavorings later.

Southern Comfort® A liqueur with a neutral spirit base and peach and almond flavors.

Strawberry Liqueur A sweet strawberry flavored liqueur usually 30–50 proof (15–25% alcohol) with added sugar.

Tequila A type of mescal that is made only from the blue agave plant in the region surrounding Tequila, a town in the Mexican state of Jalisco. Tequila is made in many different styles, with the difference between them dependent on how long the distillate has been aged before being bottled.

Tia Maria® A brand of coffee-flavored liqueur from Jamaica. Tia Maria® is Jamaican rum–based and flavored with spices.

Triple Sec A highly popular flavoring agent in many drinks, triple sec is the best known form of curaçao, a liqueur made from the skins of the curaçao orange.

Vodka A neutral spirit that can be distilled from almost anything that will ferment (grain, potatoes, grapes, corn, and beets). It is distilled multiple times, filtered to remove impurities, then diluted with water to bring the alcohol content down before it is bottled. Vodka is sold in a wide variety of flavors, from bison grass to watermelon.

Wild Turkey® A brand of Kentucky straight bourbon whiskey produced by the Austin Nichols Distilling Co. in Lawrenceburg, Kentucky. Wild Turkey is commonly bottled at IOI proof.

Whiskey (or Whisky) A beverage distilled from fermented grain and aged in oak casks. The location, grain, type of oak, and length of the aging all affect the flavor of the whiskey. Whiskey is spelled with an "e" in Ireland and the United States and without the "e" everywhere else. There are four major regions where whiskey is produced: Ireland, Scotland, Canada, and the United States. Each has a different style that imparts a distinctive flavor.

THE DRINKS

ADAMS BOMB

SHOT

1 part **Jägermeister**

1 part **gin**

DROP

¼ pint **orange juice**

¼ pint **club soda**

SHOT
2 parts Southern Comfort

2 parts amaretto

1 part sloe gin

DROP
½ pint Red Bull

ALABAMA BOMBER

SHOT

1 part **vodka**

1 part **amaretto**

1 part **orange juice**

DROP

1/2 pint **Red Bull**

ALMOND DRIVER

APPLE CIDER SLIDER

SHOT
1 part
sour apple–
flavored
schnapps

DROP
½ pint beer

APPLE PIE HOLE

SHOT

4 parts sour apple-flavored schnapps

1 part cinnamon schnapps

DROP

½ pint Red Bull

SHOT

2 parts sour apple-flavored schnapps

2 parts heavy cream

1 part cinnamon schnapps

DROP

½ pint Red Bull

APPLE PIE HOLE A LA MODE

B-52 BOMBER

SHOT

1 part coffee liqueur

1 part Irish Cream liqueur

1 part amaretto

DROP

½ pint Red Bull

BANANABOMB

SHOT
1 part 151-proof rum
1 part crème
de banana

DROP
½ pint Red Bull

SHOT
1 part scotch
1 part Irish
Cream liqueur

DROP
½ pint Guinness Stout

BELFAST
CAR BOMB

BETON

SHOT
1 part scotch
1 part vodka

DROP
1 pint beer

SHOT
1 part sambuca
1 part blackberry liqueur

DROP
½ pint Red Bull

BLACK JELLY BOMB

BLACK LICORICE

SHOT
1 part
Jägermeister®

DROP
½ pint lemon - lime soda

BLOODY MESS

SHOT

1 part **vodka**

1 part **tomato juice**

Dash **Tabasco® sauce**

Dash **Worcestershire sauce**

DROP

½ pint **beer**

SHOT
1 part Irish Cream liqueur

1 part butterscotch schnapps

DROP
½ pint Red Bull

BLOWING BUTTER

SHOT

2 parts peach schnapps

1 part heavy cream

DROP

½ pint beer

BLUSHING SPEW

BOMBAY BOMBSHELL

SHOT
2 parts **gin**

1 part **lime juice**

DROP
½ pint **tonic water**

BOMBER

SHOT
1 part tequila

DROP
½ pint light beer

SHOT
2 parts Midori
1 part vodka

DROP
½ pint sake

BONZAI

BOOTLEG BOOSTER

SHOT
1 part un-aged corn whiskey
1 part Southern Comfort

DROP
½ pint beer

BOOTY SHAKER

SHOT
1 part **coconut-flavored rum**

1 part **spiced rum**

1 part **melon liqueur**

DROP
1/2 pint **Red Bull**

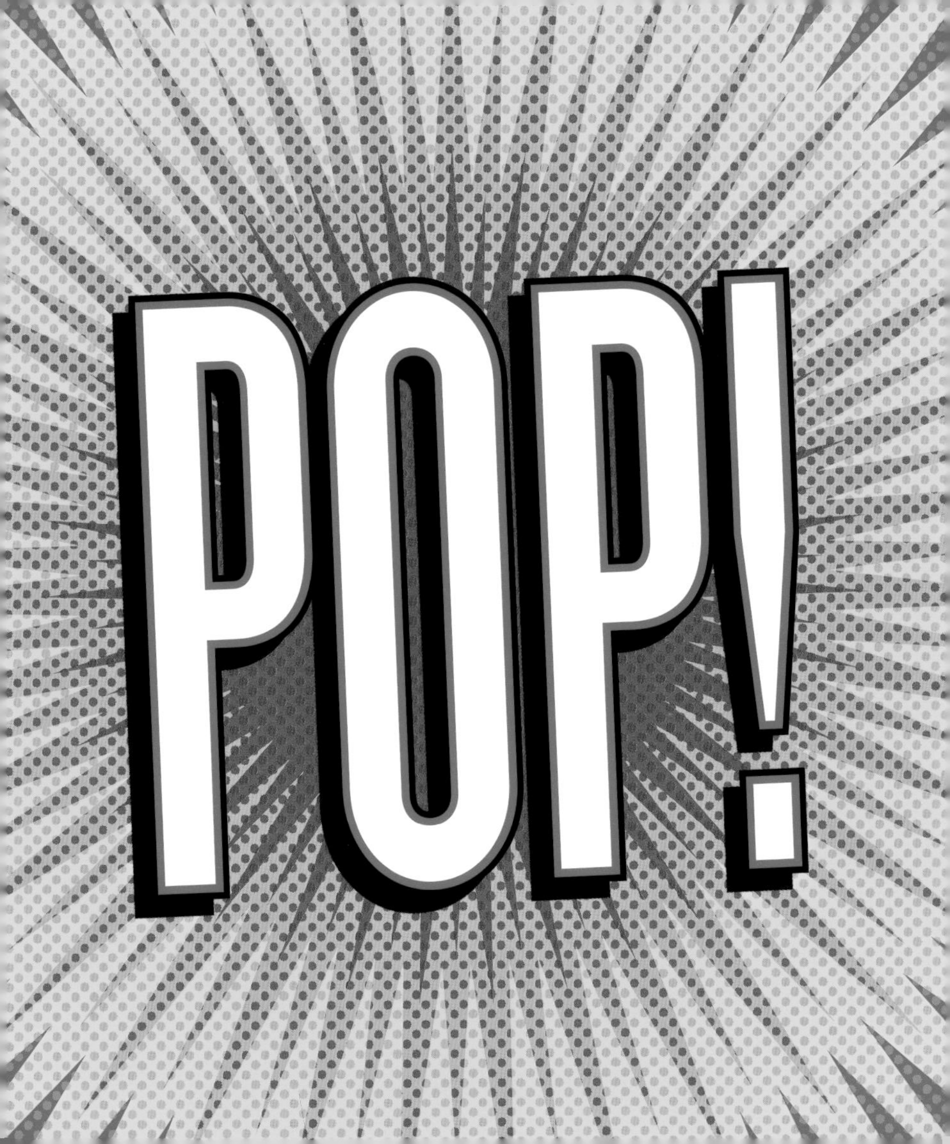
POP!

BOSTON BOMBER

SHOT

1 part gin

1 part apricot brandy

Dash grenadine

Dash lemon juice

DROP

½ pint Red Bull

SHOT

1 part **coconut-flavored rum**

1 part **amaretto**

DROP

½ pint **iced coffee**

BOUNCE BACK

BOWL HUGGER BOMB

SHOT

1 part tequila

1 part rum

1 part gin

1 part vodka

DROP

¼ pint Red Bull

¼ pint orange juice

SHOT
1 part vodka
1 part coffee liqueur

DROP
½ pint club coda

BRAIN BOMB

SHOT

1 part **151-proof rum**

1 part **crème de banana**

1 part **triple sec**

DROP

½ pint **Red Bull**

BRAIN DAMAGER

BRASS BALLS BOMBER

SHOT
1 part **Grand Marnier**

1 part **peach schnapps**

1 part **pineapple juice**

DROP
½ pint **Red Bull**

BRITISH SNAFU

SHOT
1 part **scotch**

1 part **gin**

DROP
½ pint **Red Bull**

SHOT
1 part gin

1 part vermouth

1 part orange juice

DROP
1/2 pint Red Bull

BRONX BOMBER

BUBBLE TROUBLE

SHOT

1 part **Southern Comfort**

1 part **crème de banana**

1 part **grenadine**

1 part **milk**

DROP

½ pint **Red Bull**

BULLING OF THE RUNS

SHOT
1 part tequila

DROP
½ pint Red Bull

SHOT
1 part coffee liqueur

1 part cherry-flavored schnapps

DROP
½ pint Red Bull

BUSTED CHERRY BOMB

CACTUS-FLOWER
BOMB

SHOT

1 part **tequila**

1 part **blue curaçao**

1 part **amaretto**

1 part **vanilla schnapps**

DROP

½ pint **Corona® beer**

CALIFORNIA SURFER WIPEOUT

SHOT

1 part **Jägermeister**

1 part **coconut - flavored rum**

1 part **pineapple juice**

DROP

½ pint **Red Bull**

CANNON BALL!

SHOT

1 part **melon liqueur**

1 part **crème de banana**

1 part **cranberry juice**

DROP

½ pint **club soda**

CAR BOMB

SHOT
1 part whiskey
1 part Irish
Cream liqueur

DROP
½ pint Guinness Stout

SHOT
1 part vodka
1 part cherry-
flavored schnapps

DROP
½ pint Red Bull

CHERRY BOMB

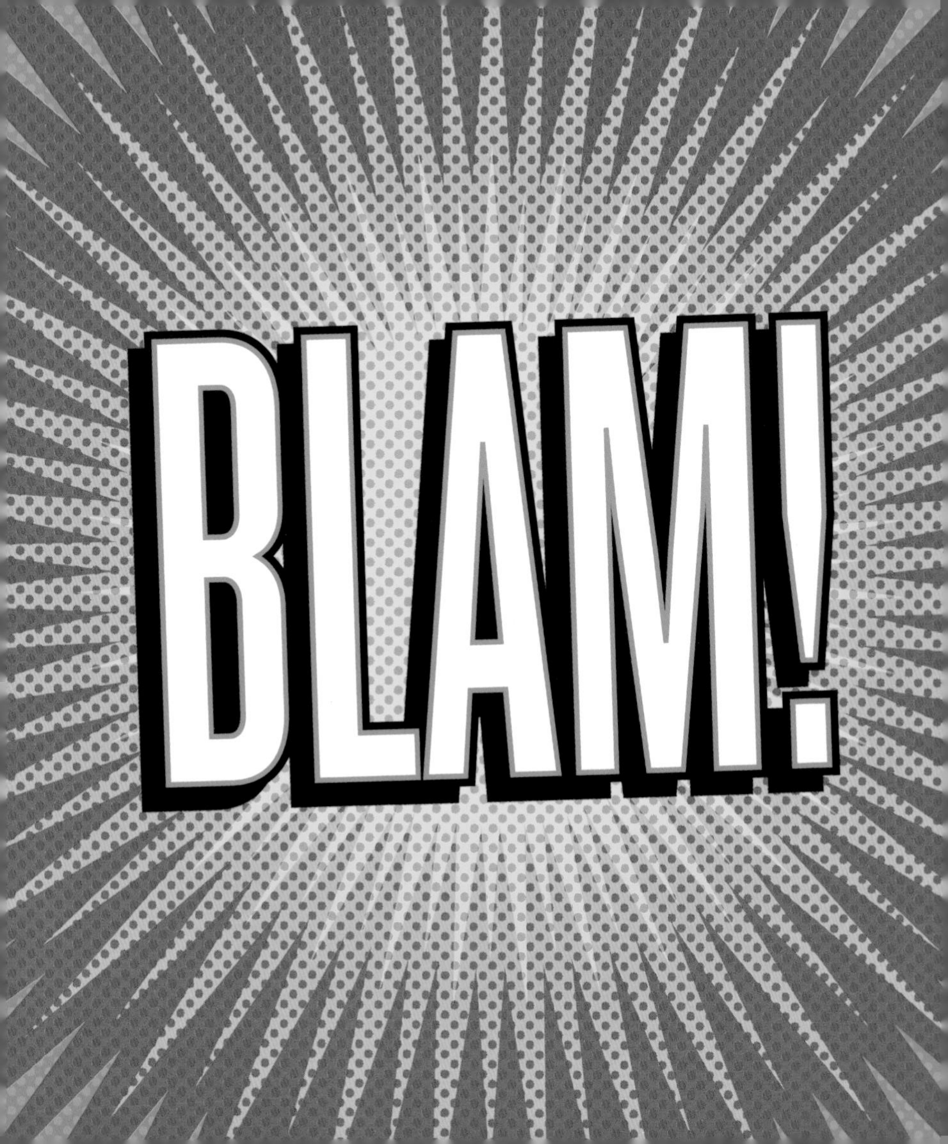
BLAM!

CHOCOLATE-COVERED CHERRY BOMB

SHOT

1 part **vodka**

1 part **cherry-flavored schnapps**

1 part **chocolate liqueur**

DROP

½ pint **Red Bull**

CHRISTMAS CRUTCH

SHOT
1 part peppermint schnapps

DROP
½ pint Red Bull

SHOT
1 part Jägermeister

DROP
½ pint Woodchuck® Hard Cider

CHUCK JAGER

COCO BOMBO

SHOT

1 part chocolate liqueur

1 part coconut-flavored rum

1 part heavy cream

DROP

½ pint Red Stripe® beer

CRANBERRY BOMBER

SHOT

1 part vodka

1 part cranberry juice

1 part orange juice

DROP

½ pint Red Bull

CUBANISMO

SHOT
1 part
light rum

DROP
½ pint
ginger ale

DA BOMB

SHOT

1 part sour apple-flavored schnapps

1 part peach schnapps

1 part crème de banana

DROP

½ pint Red Bull

DAS AUTOBAHM

SHOT
1 part **Jägermeister**

1 part **Rumple Minze**

DROP
½ pint **Red Bull**

DEEP BLUE SEA

SHOT
1 part blue curaçao

DROP
1/2 pint Red Bull

SHOT
1 part Jägermeister

DROP
1/2 pint root beer

DETTO BOMB

DEVIL'S DILEMMA

SHOT

1 part **dark rum**

1 part **light rum**

1 part **apricot brandy**

1 part **pineapple juice**

Dash **grenadine**

DROP

½ pint **Red Bull**

SHOT
1 part **Jack Daniel's**

1 part **Southern Comfort**

DROP
1/2 pint **Mountain Dew**

DEW ME PROUD

DIVE BOMBER

SHOT
1 part amaretto

1 part root beer schnapps

DROP
½ pint beer

DIXIE BOMB

SHOT
1 part coconut-flavored rum

1 part crème de banana

1 part limoncello

1 part pineapple juice

DROP
½ pint club soda

DOCTOR JAGER

SHOT

1 part
Jägermeister

DROP

½ pint
Dr. Pepper®

SHOT

3 parts
amaretto
1 part
151-proof rum

DROP

½ pint beer

DOCTOR PEPPER

DROPPING ACID

SHOT
1 part **151-proof rum**
1 part **Wild Turkey**

DROP
½ pint **beer**

EYE OF THE TIGER

SHOT

1 part **Southern Comfort**

1 part **raspberry liqueur**

1 part **sour apple-flavored schnapps**

DROP

½ pint **club soda**

SHOT

1 part tequila

1 part Jack Daniel's

1 part vodka

1 part Tabasco® sauce

DROP

½ pint beer

FIRE BOMB

FLAMING ANUS

SHOT
1 part tequila

1 part sambuca

1 part
Tabasco sauce

DROP
½ pint beer

FLAMING CORNHOLIO

SHOT
1 part cinnamon schnapps

DROP
1 part Jack Daniel's
3 parts orange juice

SHOT
1 part 151-proof rum (lit on fire)

DROP
½ pint beer

FLAMING DEPTH CHARGE

FLAMING DR. PEPPER

SHOT
1 part 151-proof rum (lit on fire)

3 parts raspberry liqueur

DROP
½ pint beer

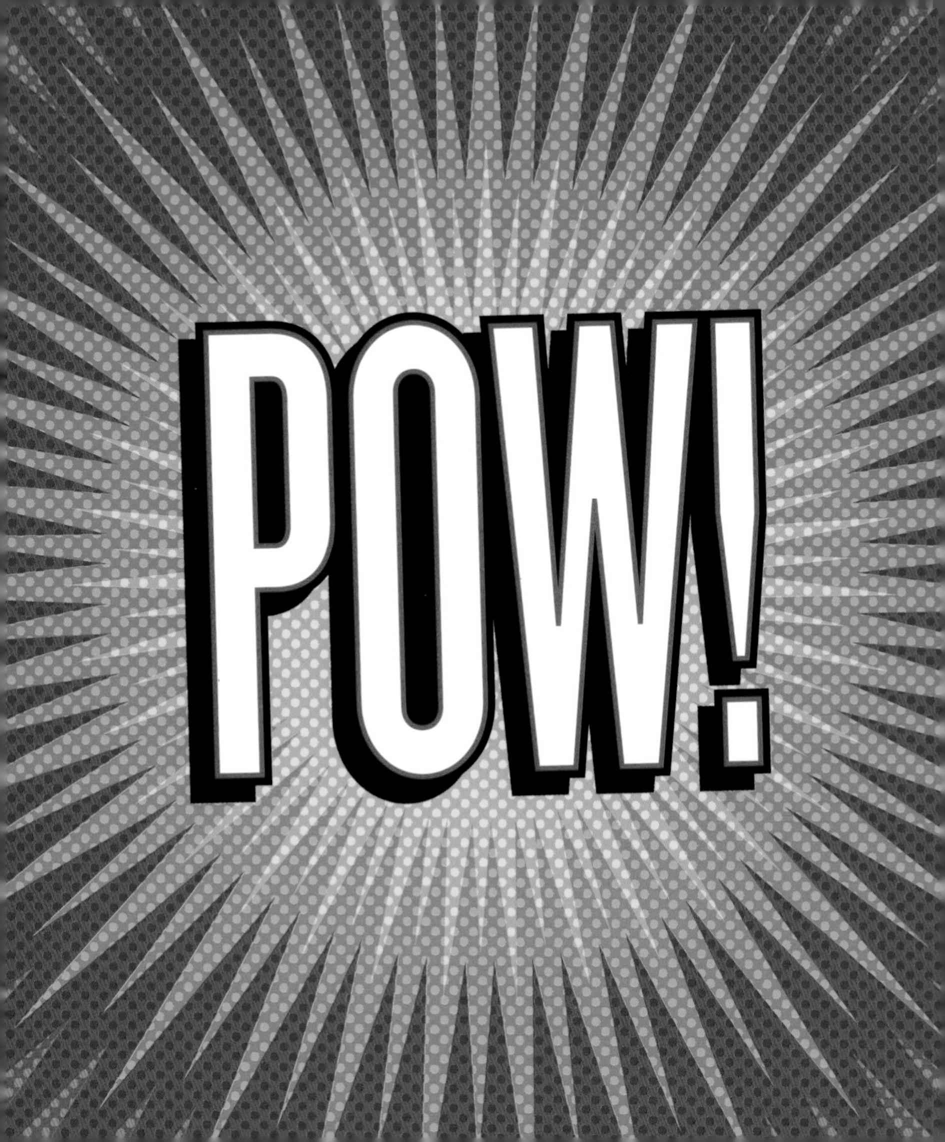
POW!

SHOT

3 parts amaretto

1 part 151-proof rum (lit on fire)

DROP

½ pint beer

FLAMING DR. PEPPER

(Alternate)

FUZZY IRANIAN

SHOT
1 part peach schnapps

DROP
½ pint beer

SHOT
1 part peach schnapps
1 part vodka

DROP
½ pint Mountain Dew

FUZZY PEACH BOMB

GERMAN CAR BOMB

SHOT
**1 part
Jägermeister**

DROP
**¹/₂ pint
Heineken®
beer**

GERMAN CHOCOLATE BOMB

SHOT

1 part chocolate liqueur

1 part cherry-flavored schnapps

DROP

1/2 pint Red Bull

SHOT
1 part **gin**

DROP
½ pint **beer**

GIN AND BEAR IT

GINGERBREAD BOMB

SHOT
1 part Irish Cream liqueur

1 part cinnamon schnapps

1 part butterscotch schnapps

DROP
½ pint ginger ale

GREEN BASTARD

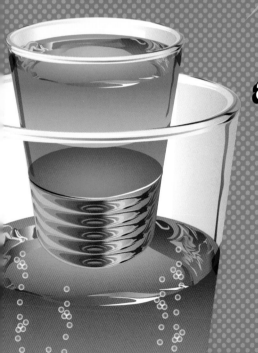

SHOT
1 part **sour apple-flavored schnapps**

1 part **blue curaçao**

DROP
½ pint **beer**

GREEN GOBLIN

SHOT

1 part sour apple-flavored schnapps

1 part vodka

DROP

½ pint Red Bull

SHOT

1 part raspberry liqueur

1 part crème de banana

1 part grapefruit juice

DROP

½ pint Red Bull

GUMMY BOMB

GUT BUSTER

SHOT
1 part rum
1 part Tabasco sauce

DROP
½ pint beer

SHOT
1 part Irish whiskey

DROP
¼ pint Woodchuck Hard Cider
¼ pint Guinness Stout

HAIRBALL

HAND GRENADE

SHOT
1 part pineapple-flavored vodka

DROP
½ pint Red Bull

SHOT
1 part Bärenjäger Honey Liqueur

1 part Jägermeister

DROP
½ pint Red Bull

HONEY BADGER

IRISH CAR BOMB

SHOT
1 part Irish whiskey
1 part coffee liqueur
1 part Irish Cream liqueur

DROP
1/2 pint Guinness Stout

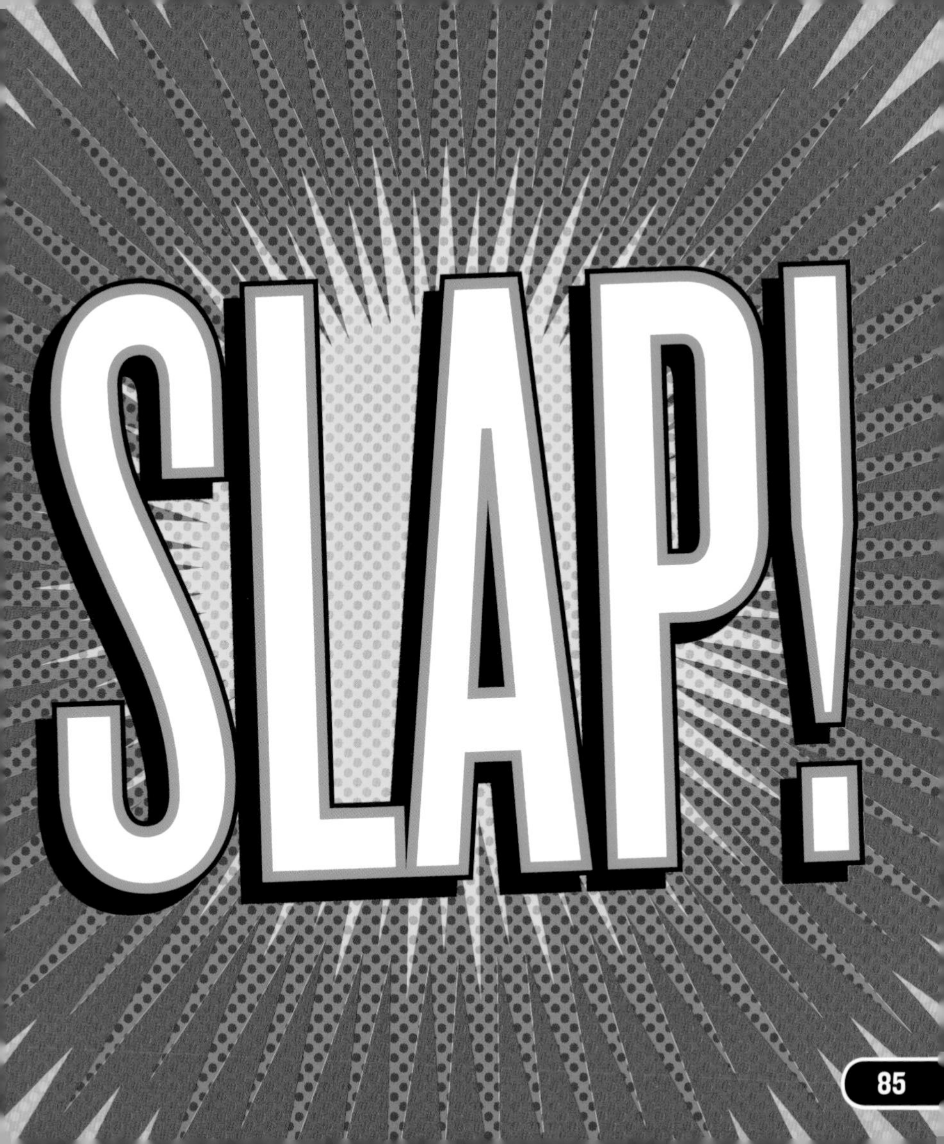
SLAP!

ISLAND CAR BOMB

SHOT

1 part **dark rum**

1 part **cherry brandy**

1 part **pineapple juice**

DROP

½ pint **Red Bull**

JÄGER BEER BOMB

SHOT
1 part **Jägermeister**

DROP
½ pint **beer**

SHOT
1 part **Jägermeister**

DROP
½ pint **Red Bull**

JÄGER BOMB

JÄGER SPLASH

SHOT
1 part **Jägermeister**

DROP
½ pint **V8® Splash**
(any flavor)

SHOT
1 part **dark rum**
1 part **coffee liqueur**

DROP
½ pint **ginger beer**

JAMAICAN CAR BOMB

KAMIKAZE DIVE

SHOT
1 part **vodka**

1 part **triple sec**

1 part **lime juice**

DROP
½ pint **Red Bull**

KISS OF DEATH

SHOT
1 part **whiskey**
1 part **151-proof rum**

DROP
½ pint **Red Bull**

SHOT
1 part **Licor 43**
(Cuarenta y Tres)

DROP
½ pint **Red Bull**

LA BOMBA

LONG ISLAND CAR BOMB

SHOT
1 part **rum**

1 part **vodka**

1 part **tequila**

1 part **gin**

1 part **triple sec**

1 part **sour mix**

DROP
½ pint **cola**

LUNCH BOX

SHOT
1 part amaretto

DROP
¼ pint beer

¼ pint orange juice

SHOT
1 part
melon liqueur

DROP
¼ pint
pineapple juice

¼ pint
orange juice

MELON SQUISHY

MEXICAN GUT BUSTER

SHOT
1 part tequila

1 part Tabasco sauce

DROP
½ pint Corona beer

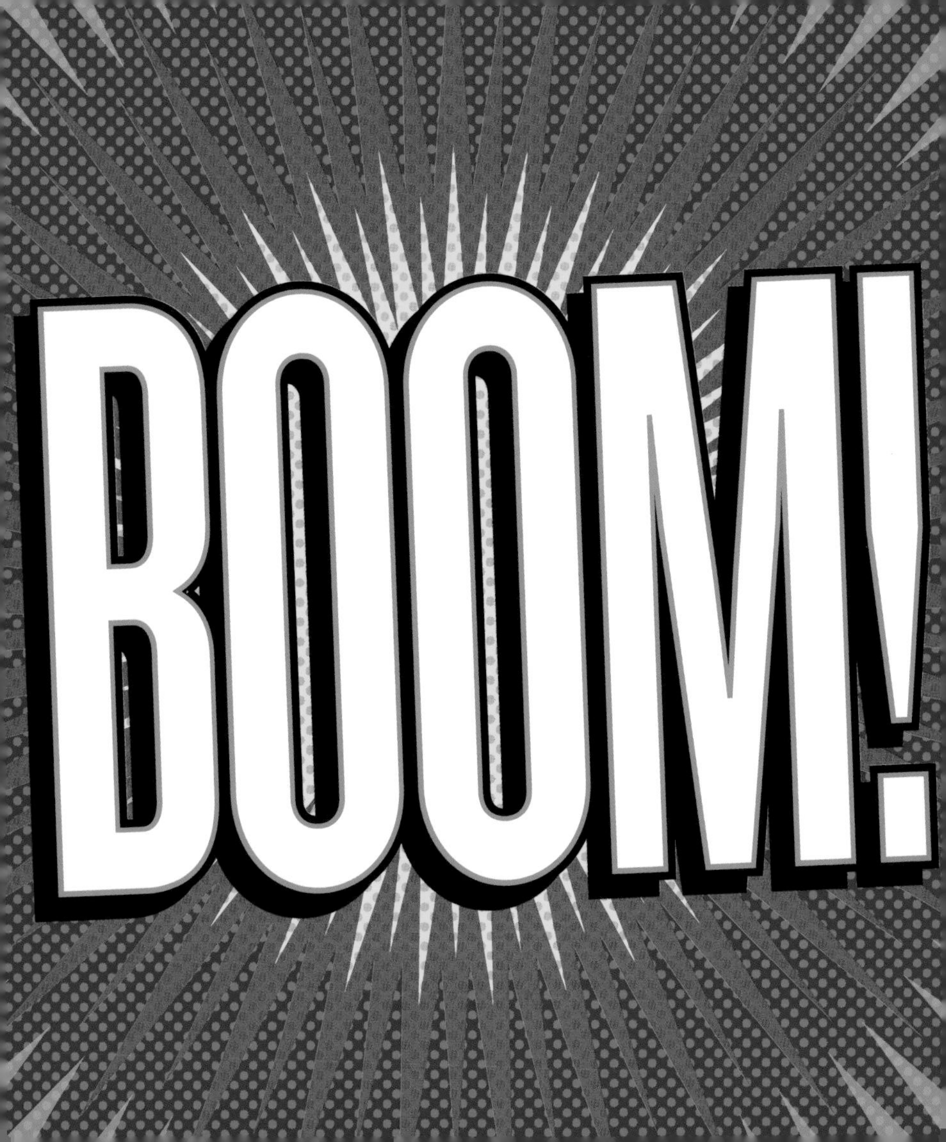
BOOM!

MEXICAN HILLBILLY

SHOT
1 part Jack Daniel's

DROP
½ pint Corona beer

SHOT
1 part peppermint schnapps

DROP
½ pint Mountain Dew

MINTY GUM SHOT

MOUNTAIN DEW

SHOT
1 part melon liqueur

DROP
¼ pint beer
¼ pint lemon-lime soda

SHOT
1 part Jägermeister

DROP
½ pint Mountain Dew

MOUNTAIN MEISTER

NUCLEAR BOMB

SHOT
1 part blue curaçao

3 parts melon liqueur

DROP
½ pint Red Bull

NUKED RUSSIAN

SHOT
1 part **Kahlúa**

1 part **vodka**

DROP
½ pint **milk**

SHOT

1 part **vodka**

1 part **lemon-flavored rum**

1 part **melon liqueur**

DROP

½ pint **Red Bull**

OLD DIRTY BOMB

PABST SMIR

SHOT
1 part Smirnoff® vodka

DROP
½ pint Pabst Blue Ribbon® beer

SHOT
1 part peppermint schnapps

DROP
½ pint beer

PEPPERMINT DEPTH CHARGE

PINK FUZZY EXPLOSION

SHOT
2 parts peach schnapps

1 part grenadine

DROP
½ pint Red Bull

RED DEVIL

SHOT
1 part **Southern Comfort**

1 part **crème de banana**

1 part **grenadine**

DROP
½ pint **Red Bull**

ROOT BEER BARREL

SHOT
1 part root beer schnapps

DROP
½ pint beer

SHOT
1 part vodka

DROP
½ pint beer

RUSSIAN BOILERMAKER

SAKE BOMB

SHOT
1 part sake

DROP
1/2 pint beer

SHOT
1 part sambuca

DROP
1/2 pint beer

SAMBUCA
DEPTH CHARGE

SAMUEL JACKSON

SHOT
1 part 151-proof rum

DROP
½ pint Samuel Adams Boston Lager®

SCHOOL BUS

SHOT
1 part amaretto

DROP
¼ pint beer

¼ pint orange juice

SCREAMING PURPLE JESUS

SHOT
1 part vodka

DROP
½ pint grape soda

SHOT
1 part amaretto

DROP
¼ pint beer
¼ pint cola

SERGEANT PEPPER

SHOOT THE ROOT

SHOT
1 part root beer schnapps

DROP
1/2 pint beer

SHOT

1 part vanilla-flavored vodka

1 part orange-flavored vodka

1 part milk

DROP

½ pint Red Bull

SHOOTING CREAMSICLE

SKY DIVE

SHOT
2 parts blue curaçao
1 part heavy cream

DROP
½ pint Red Bull

SLOW COMFORTABLE BOMB

SHOT

1 part **Southern Comfort**

1 part **sloe gin**

DROP

½ pint **orange soda**

SOCO BOMB

SHOT
3 parts **Southern Comfort**
1 part **lime juice**

DROP
½ pint **Red Bull**

SHOT
1 part **Cointreau**

DROP
½ pint **Red Bull**

SKITTLE BOMB
(or C-BOMB)

STRAWBEERY

SHOT
1 part strawberry liqueur

DROP
½ pint beer

SHOT
1 part Jägermeister

DROP
½ pint beer

SUBMARINE

TENNESSEE BOILERMAKER

SHOT
1 part **Jack Daniel's**

DROP
½ pint **beer**

SHOT
1 part **tequila**

DROP
½ pint **lemon-lime soda**

TEQUILA POPPER XXL

THE OBAMA

SHOT
2 parts orange-flavored vodka

1 part orange juice

DROP
½ pint Red Bull

THREE WISE ASSES

SHOT

1 part **Jose Cuervo® tequila**

1 part **Jack Daniel's**

1 part **Johnny Walker® Scotch**

DROP

1/2 pint **Red Bull**

TIJUANA CAR BOMB

SHOT
1 part tequila

DROP
½ pint beer

SHOT
1 part blue curaçao
1 part melon liqueur

DROP
½ pint Red Bull

TIME BOMB

TNT

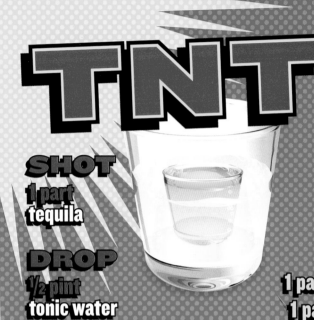

SHOT
1 part
tequila

DROP
½ pint
tonic water

SHOT
1 part Hennessy
1 part Hypnotiq

DROP
½ pint Heineken beer

TRIPLE H

VEGAS BOMB

SHOT
1 part whiskey

1 part peach schnapps

1 part coconut-flavored rum

Dash cranberry juice

DROP
½ pint Red Bull

WET AND MESSY

SHOT

1 part **Southern Comfort**

1 part **coconut-flavored rum**

1 part **cranberry juice**

1 part **pineapple juice**

DROP

½ pint **lemon-lime soda**

WHOLE IN A BUCKET

SHOT
1 part **Southern Comfort**

SHOT
1 part **amaretto**

DROP
½ pint **cranberry juice cocktail**

DROP
¼ pint **orange juice**
¼ pint **beer**

WISCONSIN LUNCH BOX

INDEX
By drink names